What Would Wonder Woman Do?

Library of Congress Cataloging-in-
Publication Data:

Colón, Suzan.
  What would Wonder Woman do? : an
Amazon's guide to the working world / by
Suzan Colón and Jennifer Traig.
     p. cm.
  ISBN-10: 0-8118-5177-X
  ISBN-13: 978-0-8118-5177-0
  1. Work—Humor. 2. Women employees—
Humor. I. Traig, Jennifer. II. Title.

  PN6231.W644C65 2007
  650.1082—dc22

  2006023557

Manufactured in China

Designed by **HENRY QUIROGA**

Distributed in Canada by
Raincoast Books
9050 Shaughnessy Street
Vancouver, British Columbia
V6P 6E5

10 9 8 7 6 5 4 3 2 1

Chronicle Books LLC
680 Second Street
San Francisco, California
94107

www.chroniclebooks.com

Contents

...NOW BACK
TO WORK!

- INTRODUCTION -

IF YOU'VE EVER HAD TO GET YOUR BOSS
ONE TOO MANY CUPS OF COFFEE . . .

IF YOU'VE EVER HAD TO STAND IN LINE
TO MAKE A COPY, ONLY TO FIND THAT
THERE'S NO PAPER OR TONER . . .

IF YOU'VE EARNED YOUR DEGREE,
ONLY TO FIND THAT YOU'RE EARNING LESS
THAN THE GUY WHO MAKES YOUR
DOUBLE-SCRAMBLED-ON-A-ROLL-WITH-CHEESE
AT THE CORNER DINER . . .

IF YOU'VE EVER ANSWERED YOUR HOME PHONE,
"HOW MAY I HELP YOU?" . . .

IF YOU'RE SPENDING YOUR SATURDAYS
CATCHING UP ON DATA ENTRY INSTEAD
OF SAVING THE UNIVERSE OR HITTING
THE BOOT SALES . . .

IF YOU'RE SO SICK OF THE PHRASE
"THINK OUTSIDE THE BOX" THAT YOU
WANT TO FEED THE BOX INTO
THE PAPER SHREDDER . . .

IF YOU'VE EVER WANTED TO MOVE
BOULDERS INSTEAD OF PUSHING PAPERS . . .

. . . THEN MAYBE IT'S TIME TO GO
FROM BEING A PLAIN WORKING
FEMALE TO BEING A FABULOUS
WORKING WONDER WOMAN.

ALL RIGHT, TAKE THIS LETTER. DEAR SIR, DISREGARDINGTHELETHAL LASSITUDESUPERINDUCEDBYTOXICINFUSIONSOFCARBONMONOXIDE FOLLOWINGCEREBRALCONCUSSIONSCAUSEDBYINVOLUNTARYABSOR TIONSOFHYDROCYANICSHELLEXPLOSIONDIFFUSIONS- ETC.,ETC.

THE SMARTY! HE'S THROWING THE DICTIONARY AT ME AT THE RATE OF 160 WORDS A MINUTE, BUT I'LL SHOW HIM!

ER—AM I DICTATING TOO FAST?

OH NO, SIR! I GOT EVERY WORD! I'LL TYPE IT FOR YOU.

FUNDS S...

WANTED: ASSISTANT/GAL FRIDAY/OC... TO WORK CLOSELY WITH U.S. ARMY OFFICER. MUST BE BEAUTIFUL AS A... AS ATHENA, STRONG AS HERCULES MERCURY, AND ABLE TO RECEIVE M... AND RUN THE OFFICE. MUST BE W... HOURS, LATE NIGHTS, WEEKENDS... MUST ALSO GO ON OCCASIONAL... ACTUALLY SECRET MISSIONS.

APPLY TO MAJOR STEVE TR...

SIONAL SPY
LLIGENCE
RODITE, WISE
WIFTER THAN
TAL MESSAGES
NG TO WORK LONG
AJOR HOLIDAYS;
ATES" THAT ARE

OR, C/O U.S. ARMY.

YOU'VE SCANNED THE WANT ADS, you've pored through the postings, and you've finally found a job you want! Whether it's as a dental technician or as the only female member of the Justice League, the only thing standing between you and your 401(k) is the job interview.

Job interviews are as much fun as paying off parking tickets and they make even a super heroine want to jump in her invisible jet and fly far away. But unless your dream job is "hobo" or "heiress," you'll just have to get through it. And you can. You've survived high school P.E., home perms, flat tires, and some really, really bad blind dates. You can *definitely* handle this. Here's how to handle your job interview the Wonder Woman way.

THE RÉSUMÉ

The first part of the interview process is, of course, your résumé. Proper assessment of your skills is key. Wonder Woman rarely doubts her abilities, and you shouldn't either. On a single sheet of high-quality résumé paper, confidently list your skills, degrees, and job history. No fancy fonts or fibs. But it's OK to brag a little. If you're an Excel whiz, say so. If you're able to subdue super-villains, mention your "excellent people skills."

Other qualities worth mentioning:

- *ABILITY TO OPERATE SWITCHBOARD, WIRELESS ROUTER, MENTAL RADIO, ETC.*

- *EXCEPTIONAL COMMUNICATION SKILLS, INCLUDING ABILITY TO GET PEOPLE TO TELL THE TRUTH VIA USE OF A GOLDEN LASSO*

- *SPEED TYPING AND DICTATION*

- *SUPERHUMAN STRENGTH*

- *FLUENCY IN ANOTHER LANGUAGE*

- *LIFESAVING OR UNIVERSE-SAVING EXPERIENCE (OR BOTH)*

- *PILOT'S LICENSE (COMMERCIAL, HOBBY, INVISIBLE)*

Wonder Woman

BEAUTY

WISDOM

APHRODITE:-

Most beautiful of all, Aphrodite was the Greek Goddess of Love and Beauty. Born of the sea foam near the Island of Cyprus, she inspired all mortal lovers and protected them, binding men in the chains of love and beauty, forged by her husband, Vulcan, the blacksmith God!

HERCULES:-

The God of Strength was half-mortal and half-God! When a mere child, he strangled two fierce serpents sent to slay him. He performed twelve labors requiring prodigious strength and upon his earthly death, was taken to Mount Olympus to dwell among the Gods ever after.

ATHENA:-

Born from the head of Zeus, Father of all Greek Gods, Athena became the Goddess of Wisdom. Though she carried sword and spear to protect mortals from the evils of ignorance, she offered peace as her greatest gift to mankind. Her symbol was the olive branch, representing peace and plenty.

MERCURY:-

Known to the ancient Greeks as Hermes, God of speed, this gay mischievous young blade who could make himself invisible with his winged cap and transport himself in a flash with his winged sandals, always carried with him his sceptre of speed, two serpents entwined about a winged shaft.

Who is she?

WHERE does she come from? How did she obtain her human, yet invincible abilities?

These are the questions everyone is asking — for WONDER WOMAN has become the talk of the hour all over America!

With the beauty of Aphrodite, the wisdom of Athena, the strength of Hercules and the speed of Mercury, this glamorous Amazon Princess flashes vividly across America's horizon from that mysterious Paradise Isle, where women rule supreme

NO.

STRENGTH

SPEED

YOUR NAME HERE

123 Main Street

Anytown, USA 98765

emailme@myemail.com

YES.

SUMMARY

- Ten years of progressive customer service experience
- Exceptional organizational and leadership skills
- Thorough planner with the ability to initiate and complete planned projects
- Thrive on change and tight deadlines
- Track record of completing projects on time and under budget

COMPUTER SKILLS

MS Office Suite, ERP, SAP, Oracle 8.1, Data Star

PROFESSIONAL EXPERIENCE

WESTERN EASTERNERS, INC. San Francisco, CA   1992–present

Customer Service Manager

Supervised department of twelve employees. Directed the development of a successful and effective customer service department. Resolved serious customer service and collection problems through process implementation and effective management.

- Reorganized and fully staffed a world-class customer service department.
- Created and implemented weekly customer service reports, improving overall customer confidence by 32% based on survey results.
- Trained employees on customer relations and win/win negotiation.
- Developed and implemented new complaint handling and reporting system

PLABADITOOK CORPORATION, Sand Spit, AZ   1985–1992

Customer Service Team Lead

Assisted Customer Service Department Manager.

- Prepared and maintained log of customer service complaints for weekly reports.
- Compiled and wrote weekly and monthly reports for customer service staff.
- Coordinated and scheduled weekly meetings for customer service staff.
- Trained and developed newly hired customer support staff.

EDUCATION

B.S., B.A. University of Phoenix, Phoenix, AZ 1991
General Business Major

PROFESSIONAL AFFILIATION

Member of International Customer Service Association
Member of San Francisco Chamber of Commerce

GETTING YOUR BOOT IN THE DOOR

If you're like Wonder Woman, you'll want to take extra measures to make sure your résumé goes straight into the "Call for an interview ASAP!" pile. You *could* take the bull by the horns, but that's likely to end in an unflattering scene with security. Sure, your potential employer would probably be impressed that you can take down three burly guys, but you might want to keep your pile-driving skills quiet until you actually have the job.

Instead, work that Rolodex. Call on any connections you might have at the company and ask for inside tips. Can they put in a good word? Any pitfalls to watch out for? Any dish to dig up? A Wonder Woman would never resort to blackmail, but she's not above a name-drop. If Aquaman's cousin's girlfriend is the head of human resources, she's definitely going to ask her pal to make a call.

THE INTERVIEW

Arrive a few minutes early so you have time to chat up the receptionists. If they like you, they might put in a good word. Compliment their clothes or crime-fighting techniques. Ask where they're from. And if you're pretty sure you once rescued them from a villain's lair, by all means, mention it. Don't beat yourself up if you get a little nervous. You're human. Even super-humans get a little tense when stock options are on the line.

You can try repeating a few affirmations:

*I AM A CONFIDENT, CAPABLE WOMAN
WHO CAN DO THE JOB.*

ANY COMPANY WOULD BE LUCKY TO HAVE ME.

I AM AS INDESTRUCTIBLE AS MY BRACELETS.

I AM ON THE SIDE OF GOOD AND GOOD IS ON MY SIDE.

*I AM A SUPER-HUMAN HERE TO SAVE THE WORLD,
AND MY SUCCESS IS PREORDAINED BY FATE.*

During the interview, your potential bosses may throw you a trick question, like asking what your weaknesses are. Good responses include:

- *"I'm a workaholic!"*

- *"I've been told I'm a perfectionist."*

- *"Sometimes, I get so wrapped up in a project, I forget to take lunch."*

- *"I come from a race of super-women whose strength, dedication, honesty, and devotion to all things good in the world are legendary. Mythical, really."*

Bad responses include:

- *"I need to leave my current job because I'm in love with my boss, which makes it difficult to do my work."*

- *"I have enemies. Powerful enemies on the side of evil who want to rule this planet. But don't worry, I can totally handle them."*

- *"I may sometimes need to leave work rather . . . suddenly. No, I can't tell you why."*

It's best to leave these details to yourself.

Wonder Woman never forgets her manners. After the interview, remember to send a thank-you note. And when appropriate, be sure to say please.

NEGOTIATING THE OFFER

Once you've aced the interview and gotten a serious offer, it's time for them to show you the big ducats. Hold out for decent ka-ching, and if they really want you, negotiate for extras. Some perks are worth asking for:

- Gym membership
- Full medical and dental
- Boot allowance
- Invisible-jet parking
- Free sodas
- Jobs for your friends

2

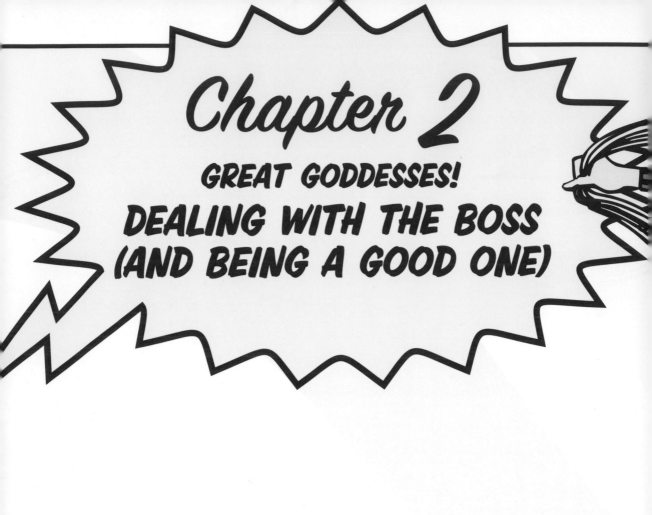

BOSSES ARE AN UNAVOIDABLE part of life. Even Wonder Woman has to answer to Major Steve Trevor. But it can be tough to take orders from a mere mortal, especially when said mortal is screaming for that overnight package and it feels like you just saved the world on your coffee break. It's enough to make an Office Amazon pile her stapler, tape dispenser, and Golden Lasso of Truth into a shoebox and head on home. We've all been there, baby, but don't despair. A Wonder Woman knows how to make the best of it.

IS THE BOSS GIVING YOU HIVES? WONDER WOMAN CAN HELP.

"DRONES of the QUEEN BEE!"

CARE AND FEEDING OF THE DOMESTICATED BOSS

IF WORK IS A THREE-RING CIRCUS, THE BOSS IS THE LION. SURE, ITS ROAR CAN BE A LITTLE SCARY, BUT IT'S EASY ENOUGH TO TRAIN AND RESPONDS WELL TO TREATS. THE OCCASIONAL FAVOR OR KIND WORD WILL HAVE THE BOSS PURRING. REMEMBER THESE SIMPLE TIPS:

Work Hard. It's obvious, but true—nothing makes a boss happy like a job well done. Do your best, take pride in your work, and put in a little overtime when necessary. People will notice.

Give Back. A little present from time to time never hurt anyone. Bring your boss the occasional scone or latte. And when you go out of town, consider picking her up a "My assistant went to Paradise Island and all I got was this lousy T-shirt" souvenir.

Make Nice. Sucking up isn't in your job description, but it doesn't hurt to flatter your boss from time to time. If you admire him, tell him so. If you're grateful for his advice, say thanks. Make sure he gets the credit when he deserves it. He may well return the favor.

BAD BOSSES

BAD BOSSES HAVE EXISTED SINCE ATTILA THE HUN, AND THEY CAN MAKE YOU HATE LIFE. NOT TO WORRY. WONDER WOMAN HAS HANDLED POWERFUL ENEMIES LIKE CIRCE AND DEVASTATION; SHE CAN CERTAINLY HANDLE A PETTY TYRANT IN A SUIT. HERE'S A GUIDE TO THE DIFFERENT TYPES OF BAD BOSSES AND HOW TO DEAL WITH THEM.

THE JOKER. This funny guy never calls you by your name. Diana is a perfectly good name, but he prefers to address you as Diana Banana, D-Dawg, or the D-Lady. Instead of good-bye, he has to say, "I'll be baaack"; instead of hello, "Heeeeeere's Johnny!" His constant comedy routines are as funny as a paper cut, but unfortunately, they're perfectly legal, and even human resources won't bat an eye. Your best response: perfect your courtesy laugh and think of something *really* funny, like the time your archenemy Circe tried to defeat you.

CATWOMAN. Sure, she seems soft and cuddly, but beware of her claws. She's climbing up the scratching post of success, and if you get in her way, she'll scratch *you.* Your best defense: document everything. She's not above lying to get you fired, so make sure you have plenty of documentation of the good work you've done. And steer clear of this catty kitty as much as possible.

AQUAMAN. As king of his domain, he tries to make everyone happy, but sometimes it feels like he's speaking to everyone in their own special language. Fortunately, you can swim around the problem. Just let him know, clearly and firmly, what you think he should do, and he'll take the bait.

SUPERMAN. A type-A guy, he needs everything to be perfect and isn't above micromanaging. Nothing escapes his X-ray vision: your punctuation, your desk accessories, even your pore size. The best way to handle him: keep him involved (even when you've got it under control all by yourself) by giving him frequent updates on your progress and asking his opinion. Hey, his heart is in the right place, but when he's on your last nerve of steel, step out for a little cathartic crime fighting or maybe a crunchy snack.

GOOD BOSS/BAD BOSS QUIZ

DO YOU HAVE A BAD BOSS? TAKE THIS QUIZ AND FIND OUT!

ON A TYPICAL DAY, MY BOSS MIGHT ASK ME TO:

1. DELIVER A REPORT ON THE COMPANY'S LONG-TERM MARKETING STRATEGY.

2. PICK UP HIS DRY CLEANING.

3. FORCE ALL HUMANS TO SURRENDER TO HIS DOMINION.

MY BOSS'S HOBBY IS:

1. GOLF.

2. SAILING.

3. CONSTRUCTING DEATH RAYS.

MY BOSS ASKS ME TO ADDRESS HIM AS:

1. SIR.

2. MISTER.

3. EVIL OVERLORD.

SCORE: ANY 3s? YOU MAY WANT TO QUIT BEFORE YOU GET FIRED—OR FLAMBÉD.

ABOVE AND BEYOND

Even if you don't have bulletproof bracelets, you can still deflect unreasonable requests with these handy responses:

Unreasonable request: I need you to babysit my kids tonight.
Response: Sure! I had plans with my motorcycle gang, but I'll just bring them along!

Unreasonable request: I'd like you to do all my holiday shopping this year.
Response: Sure. I know just the place— the Salad Dressing Outlet! Do you want pints or quarts?

Unreasonable request: We're going to need you to come in on Saturday.
Response: I'm afraid I can't. I'm in this army reserves–type thing and will be serving my country. Top secret. In fact, I've already told you too much. It's not safe. Listen, is your address listed? You might want to think about moving.

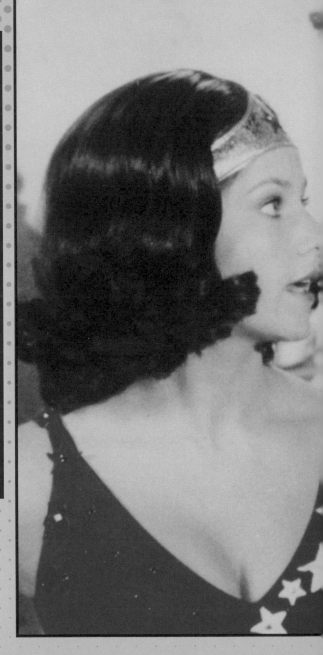

YOU WORK FOR A MAN?
HE TELLS YOU WHAT TO DO . . .
AND YOU DO IT?!

YOU'RE THE BOSS, APPLESAUCE

AND WHAT ABOUT THE DAY THAT YOU BECOME THE BOSS?

BEING PROMOTED CAN BE A PARTICULARLY DIFFICULT ADJUSTMENT FOR OFFICE AMAZONS. THERE ARE CULTURAL CONSIDERATIONS—ON PARADISE ISLAND THEY LEARNED TO DOMINATE MEN, AND TO THINK OF ALL WOMEN AS LITTLE SISTERS. THIS CAN BE A RECIPE FOR BOSSY BOSSES. TRY TO KEEP THAT IMPULSE IN CHECK.

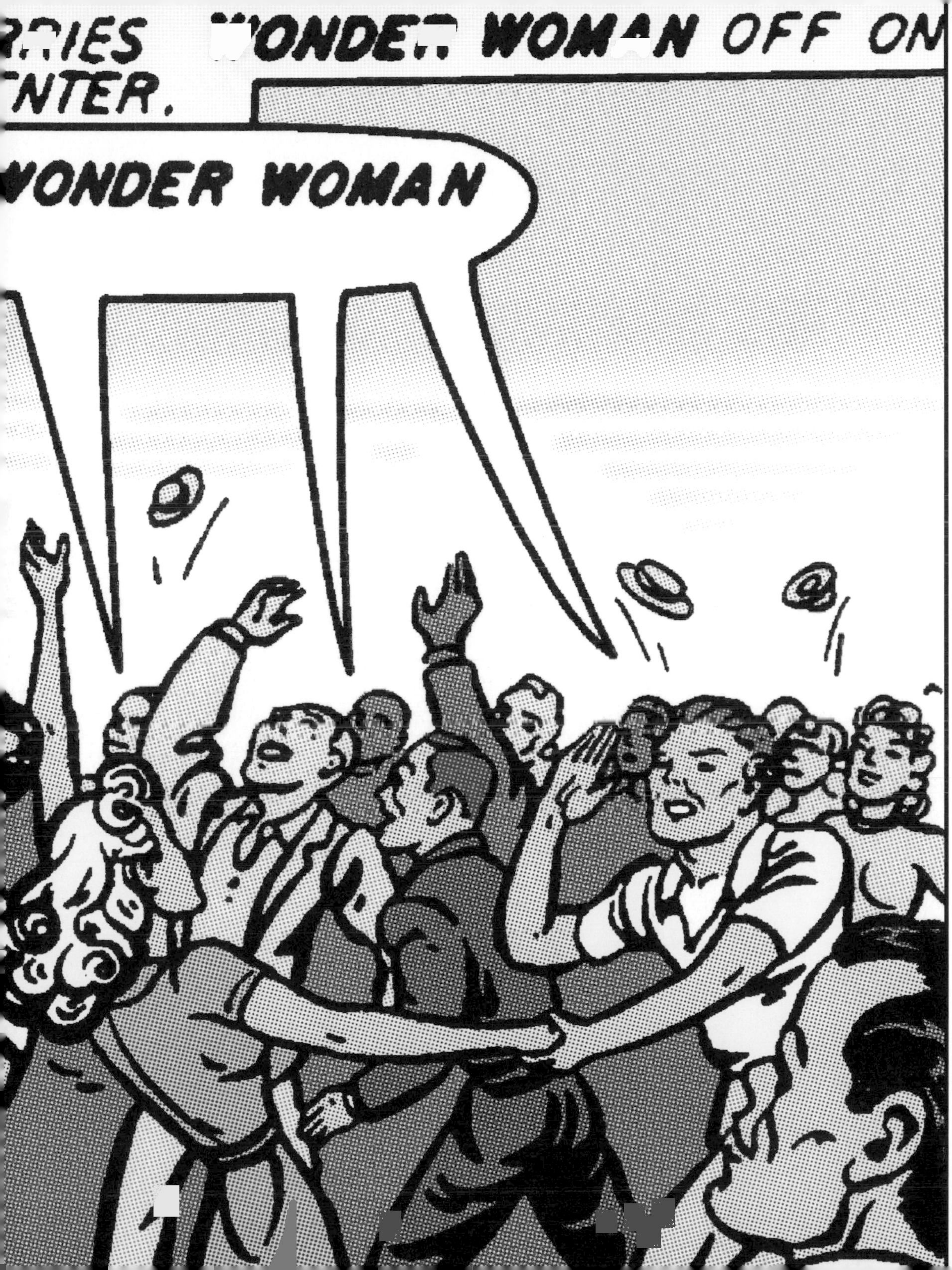
RIES WONDE WOM N OFF ON
NTER.
WONDER WOMAN

EVEN IF YOU'RE A SUPER HEROINE WHO'S USED TO FLYING SOLO, you'll have to learn how to work and play well with others.

Some co-workers are great and become super-friends outside of the office. And then there are those who sap your strength, ask too many favors, and eat all the Twizzlers. They can suck up so much of your time, they're almost as dangerous as super-villains and archcriminals. Here are a few types you should try to stay away from.

THE CHITCHATTER

Her powers: The ability to distract you from your work by endlessly shooting the breeze.

Your best defense: Utter the magical incantation, "I wish I could talk, but I'm on a deadline." Failing that: Headphones.

BE WARY OF THE CHITCHATTER.

THE DAMSEL IN DISTRESS

Her powers: Total ineptitude. This conniving co-worker seems to have constant problems, and she will seek you out and expect you to drop everything and rescue her again and again.

Your best defense: Let Blunder Woman handle her own crises—eventually she'll learn how to solve her own problems.

THE ARCHRIVAL

Her powers: A so-called healthy competitive streak that masks her true intentions: stabbing you in the back, taking your job, and otherwise besmirching your good standing in the company.

Your best defense: Be quietly superior to her in every way.

THE FLATTERER

His powers: Attractiveness, good conversation, and the ability to blind you to his real intentions and talk you out of the last jelly doughnut. He's after something, whether it's a favor, information, or more sugar.

Your best defense: Just play it cool, hot stuff.

THE KLEPTO

Her powers: An utter lack of morals. Your good Rollerball pens, your Reese's Peanut Butter Cups, the special novelty Post-its you brought in from home—she helps herself to all of it. She regards the contents of the office fridge as a free buffet, even when clearly labeled: *"Diana's egg salad. Keep out. This means you, Klepto."*

Your best defense: Backdate the expiration date on your soy milk and Lunchables, and use that locking top-desk drawer.

GIVE THOSE STICKY FINGERS SOME HANDI WIPES.

THE FRUIT BAT

Her powers: Nutty idiosyncrasies that seem to excuse her from everything. "Paranoia" is her favorite word. She can't touch the fax because it's contaminated. She can't use the copier because it emits dangerous gamma rays. She sure has her thumb on your last nerve, though.

Your best defense: Take everything with a grain of salt. Alternatively, sneeze uncontrollably when she comes near.

THE MOTHER HEN

Her powers: Smothering overinvolvement in all your affairs. Your skirt is too short; you'll catch cold. You can't keep your desk like that; you'll never find anything. You're going to send the report off looking like *that*? Let me fix it for you.

Your best defense: Roll your eyes and sigh heavily. What*ever*.

CHILL OUT, MOM.

FUN WITH YOUR CO-WORKERS

Looking for a fun way to build camaraderie? Why not form a Justice League? It's way more fun than a company picnic, and you'll fight crime *and* learn to cooperate.

THE LIFE OF A WORKING GIRL may sound appealing—regular paychecks, benefits, and the rewarding feeling you'll get from lending others a helping hand (and Hera knows they need it). But you should know that it's going to be a challenge, even with your superabilities.

Some days you can breeze into the office and greet everyone with a cheery *"¡Hola!"* and the day goes smoothly. Other days it feels like you're working for Dr. Psycho, and he's stolen all your superpowers. At times like this, it can take every bit of your Amazonian strength not to quit, pack up your tiara, and fly back to Paradise Island.

The gods may have given you superstrength, incredible intelligence, and the ability to keyboard as fast as Mercury, but in the office, these powers don't count for much without the power to schmooze, to finesse a faux pas, and to make your bosses and others look good. These are the skills a working Wonder Woman has to master, and here are some of the situations you'll need to be prepared for.

HOW TO BE LATE

WE'RE ALL PRESENT AND ACCO
THE VERY MEMBERS WHO SEN
SIGNALS TO MEET
THEM HERE !

Showing up late isn't great form, but everyone has the occasional morning mishap. A note from your mom—even if she is Queen Hippolyta—won't help, but you can handle being late the right way. Call to let them know you're on your way, and show up ready to dive into work. And be sure to have a good excuse.

EXCUSE-O-MATIC

RUNNING LATE AND NO TIME TO THINK OF A GOOD EXCUSE? USE ONE OF THESE:

FOR WONDER WOMAN	FOR MORTALS
Misplaced jet (*it's invisible*)	Car got towed
Had to defuse nuclear bomb	Had to tame bad case of bed head
Global unrest	Stomach flu
Alien invasion	Traffic jam
Hoover Dam sprung a leak	Pipes froze
Sidekick has a cold	Sick cat
Broken heel	Broken heel
Powers blocked by gamma rays	Ran out of coffee

I'LL DICTATE A
I'M A LITTLE W
ABOUT DIANA, S
SHOWN UP YET
THERE YOU ARE

IN THE OFFICE OF DIANA PRINCE - SECRETARY TO COLONEL DARNELL

BETH, YOU ARE TWO HOURS LATE FOR WORK! **WHAT HAPPENED?**

I'M SORRY-BUT I'VE JUST SAVED A GIRL FROM COMMITTING SUICIDE!

ORT. RIED HASN'T

SORRY I'M LATE. I-ER- WAS TIED UP IN TRAFFIC-

AT G2 HEADQUARTERS COLONEL DARNELL IS IN A DITHER ABOUT DIANA.

SHE'S MISSING! YOU **MUST** FIND HER—**DIANA!** WHERE'VE YOU BEEN?

FINISHING THE CRIME LEADER'S CAREER—IT ENDED, LIKE THE DREAMS OF ALL CONQUERORS, IN BITTER DEFEAT!

MEETINGS

A STRANG
OF THE
MEMBER S
TH

Most office meetings are as exciting as watching cheese mold, but they're important: they ensure you maintain good relations, keep powerful people from becoming archenemies, and can help move you up the corporate ladder. Besides, meetings are not *all* bad—the really dull ones can be more relaxing than meditation. Participate, but also do your best to keep them succinct and on point.

THAT'S TELLING HIM, *GL*! LIVE AND LET LIVE--

RIGHT! IF PEOPLE WANT TO FIGHT AND ROB AND OPPRESS OTHER PEOPLE, WE CANNOT IMPOSE OUR WILLS ON THEM! THEY HAVE RIGHTS TOO, YOU KNOW!

WILL THIS STAFF MEETING EVER END?

WHAT'S GOT INTO YOU ALL? YOU DON'T SEEM ABLE TO TELL THE DIFFERENCE BETWEEN RIGHT AND WRONG ANY-MORE!

RIGHT AND WRONG? WHO ARE **YOU** TO JUDGE WHICH IS WHICH?

EVERY HUMAN SHOULD BE MASTER OF HIS OWN DESTINY!

MEETING MEDITATION MANTRAS

Turn your next office meeting into a Zen exercise with one of Wonder Woman's meditation mantras:

- *"I am achieving a new level of calm."*

- *"I am astrally projecting myself to Paradise Island."*

- *"Wonder Woman, Wonder Woman,
  All the world's waiting for you . . ."*

- *"For each minute I spend at this meeting I get one good office karma point."*

- *"Thirty minutes to lunch. Thirty minutes to lunch. Thirty minutes to lunch."*

- *Hum Wonder Woman theme song to self.*

HOW LONG CAN I HOLD OFF THIS ONSLAUGHT?

WONDER WOMAN POWER FOODS

Being the office super heroine takes a lot of energy. Here are the snacks that get Wonder Woman through the day:

- Wonder Bread (duh)

- Almonds (high in protein, fiber, and vitamin E)

- Ambrosia (mortal substitute: fro-yo)

- Frappuccino (three of these and you, too, can fly)

THE IMPORTANCE OF THE OUT-OF-OFFICE ERRAND

I AM IN A DIMENSIONA. WORLD, WONDER WOMAN! MOTA OVER TO AMAZ!

Is it acceptable to just "nip out" for a bit during office hours? It depends. If there's a once-in-a-lifetime shoe sale and those red boots you've had your eye on are 50 percent off, then call it part of your lunch hour. They're part of your work uniform, after all. Go without guilt.

SOME ERRANDS CAN
BE DELEGATED.

THE WORKOUT ERRAND KEEPS YOUR ENERGY UP ALL DAY.

KEEP THOSE SALON APPOINTMENTS SHORT.

IF THE ENTIRE PLANET IS AT STAKE, HOWEVER, FEEL FREE TO STEP OUT AT ANY TIME.

WONDER WOMAN'S DAY PLANNER

8:00 a.m.: Arrive at work.

9:00 a.m.: Staff meeting! Entertain office mates by lifting conference table with one hand.

10:00 a.m.: Return e-mails and phone calls. Important: get back to president about your Medal of Freedom. Also: call carpenter about mantel extension for extra trophy space.

11:00 a.m.: Phone conference with the rest of the Justice League. Green Arrow won't shut up. Note: ask his receptionist to switch him to decaf.

12:00 p.m.: Spinning class (turning back hands of time doesn't undo the croissant calories, unfortunately; must burn them off the hard way).

1:00 p.m.: Save universe from imminent destruction. *Again.*

2:00 p.m.: Lasso cute UPS worker.

3:00 p.m.: Recharge infinite powers with a cappuccino.

4:00 p.m.: Debriefing with the mayor.

5:00 p.m.: Beat traffic home in invisible plane.

THAT NAUGHTY ALLIGATOR LOST YOUR PADDLES - I'LL MAKE HIM PULL US BACK WITH MY MAGIC LASSO!

GEE WHIZ! I BETCHA NO KIDS EVER GOT TOWED BY A 'GATOR BEFORE!

IT'S JUST LIKE A BEAUTIFUL DREAM!

ANYTHING FOR THE CHILDREN.

A WORD ON WORKING WONDER MOMS

If you're a working mom, you're already a Wonder Woman. You're saving the world every day. We're here to remind you that sometimes you need a little rescuing, too. You deserve some *me* time, Mama, and you shouldn't be afraid to claim it. And when your superpowers are fading, take the phone off the hook, have a friend take the kids, and treat yourself to the well-deserved restorative properties of the *WONDER NAP.*

CORPORATE LADDER? That's for mere mortals. Wonder Women like you are on a corporate escalator, fast-tracking to the corner office. It's all yours for the taking. Here's how to do it all in record time.

LEARN NEW SKILLS

Want to get ahead quickly? Show the higher-ups you're looking to improve your job performance by taking extra training. Some companies will even reimburse you for classes that will improve your job performance, so take advantage of courses that will teach you new software programs, management techniques, or the latest in hand-to-hand combat.

YOU NEVER KNOW WHAT SKILLS MIGHT COME IN HANDY.

DRESS FOR SUCCESS

A career gal on her way up needs to look the part. And if there's one thing a Wonder Woman knows, it's how to dress for success. Sometimes this means leotards, hip boots, and gold headbands. Sometimes it means herringbone. Either way, try to follow these style suggestions:

WHAT TO WEAR

Suit. Nothing looks more polished and professional, be it gabardine or spandex.

Glasses. They'll conceal the resemblance to your mortal alter ego and make you look smart.

Magic Girdle. Or, failing that, control-top hose.

Wrist Brace. It won't deflect bullets, but it will help deflect repetitive motion injuries.

YES.

NO.

WHAT NOT TO WEAR

Lasso. Unless you're applying for a rodeo position, it's probably best left at home.

Cape. Powerful and commanding but not really appropriate for the office. Try a smart trench instead.

Bodysuit. Really only appropriate for full-time super heroes and Pilates instructors. Otherwise, you probably don't want to show that much leg. An inch or two above the knee is the limit.

BE A REAL TEAM PLAYER

WHILE BOTH TEAMS WAT[CH] HER FIRST BALL AT TE[N] ALLEY!

OO-H! THAT'S TERRIBLE!

SHE'S A C[...]

A working Wonder Woman must perfect the art of getting along with others in the office, but what about being a team player after hours, too? Join the company bowling league or softball team. You'll score points with your co-workers and boss, and you might even discover a hidden talent. Show them you can be a Fun-derWoman, too!

WONDER WOMAN CONSULTS THE SCOREBOARD.
HOW 'M I DOIN'?
DOING? WOO-WOO! YOU'RE STRIKING 'EM OUT - PERFECT SCORE! ONE MORE STRIKE IN THIS LAST FRAME AND YOU MAKE 300! - AND WE WIN!
9

PREPARE FOR YOUR ANNUAL REVIEW

At your annual review you get to find out what your boss *really* thinks of your work over the past year. Maybe she will thank you for a job well done, promote you, and give you a raise to boot. (Yay! More boots!) Or she or he may come down on you with the wrath of the gods and make you wish you'd never left Paradise Island.

If it's the former, pat yourself on the back. The goddesses of the workforce have smiled upon you. But if it's the latter scenario, listen to what your boss has to say without being defensive. If you can stop a train in its tracks, ride the wind like a bird, and mentally command a robot plane, you can hear a little constructive criticism without getting all hot under the bustier. Annual reviews can be difficult, but for the love of Aphrodite, keep it together and take it like an Amazon.

WONDER WOMAN, MEANWHILE, IS REBUKED BY APHRODITE.

MY CHILD, THOU HAST DONE WONDERS IN THE WORLD OF MEN. BUT ONE ERROR NEEDS CORRECTION— THOU MUST NOT SHRINK FROM TAKING RESPONSIBILITY!

WHAT RE-SPONSIBILITY DID I FAIL TO TAKE?

HOW TO ASK FOR WHAT YOU WANT—AND GET IT

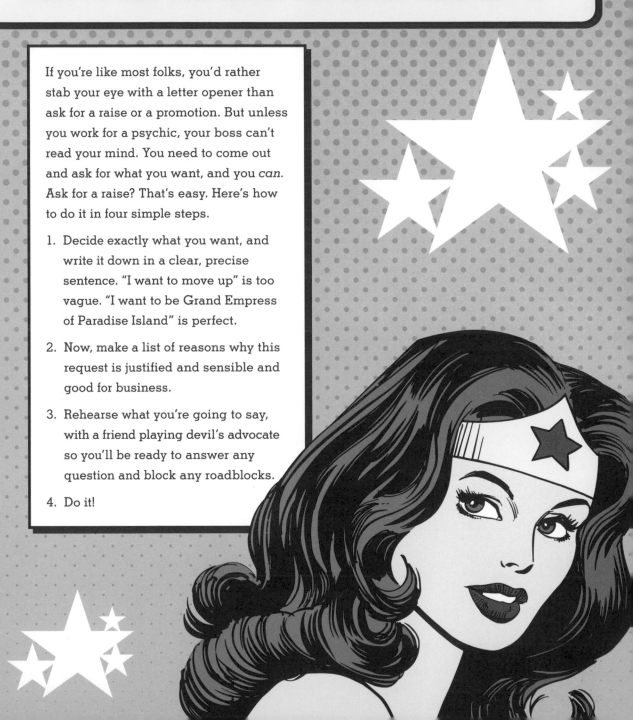

If you're like most folks, you'd rather stab your eye with a letter opener than ask for a raise or a promotion. But unless you work for a psychic, your boss can't read your mind. You need to come out and ask for what you want, and you *can*. Ask for a raise? That's easy. Here's how to do it in four simple steps.

1. Decide exactly what you want, and write it down in a clear, precise sentence. "I want to move up" is too vague. "I want to be Grand Empress of Paradise Island" is perfect.

2. Now, make a list of reasons why this request is justified and sensible and good for business.

3. Rehearse what you're going to say, with a friend playing devil's advocate so you'll be ready to answer any question and block any roadblocks.

4. Do it!

HOW TO FIND YOUR INNER WONDER WOMAN

The world loves a strong woman, and not just because she's brave enough to wear an eagle-emblazoned tube top. Take-charge women *rock*. If you feel more super zero than super hero, it's time to find your inner Wonder Woman. Try these tricks to bring her out:

- Pick a theme song that fires you up. Good choices include Helen Reddy's "I Am Woman," Christina Aguilera's "Fighter," Queen's "We Are the Champions," or pretty much anything with "na-na-na-na" for the chorus.

- Find a rallying cry. "Geronimo!" and "Cowabunga!" are classics, but you might also be motivated by "Manolo!"

- Pick your super hero name. It should probably include an adjective like *fantastic, super, ultra,* or *all-powerful.*

- Designate a sidekick. Having a junior partner makes summoning your superpowers easier.

- And finally, when all else fails: red boots really help.

YOU HANDLED ME WONDER WOMAN IF I DON'T LIKE

NOW YO YOU SEE IS YOU'V BE **A BI** IT AND BE H

CONFIDENCE BREEDS SUCCESS.

Chapter 6

SUFFERING SAPPHO!
THE PERILS OF THE OFFICE ROMANCE

Despite amazing strength and intelligence, as well as super-human skills with a Golden Lasso of Truth and online expense reports, even a working Wonder Woman may succumb to an office romance with her boss or a co-worker. Watch out, Amazon: an office romance can be a highly problematic situation. Yes, he's good looking, he's powerful, and he thinks you're a goddess. And sure, it could work out, and you and he could make quite a team. But there are no guarantees in this man's world, and if things go south, that can make for some pretty uncomfortable moments on the job.

If you decide to date the boss or one of your co-workers, here are some of the problems you may run into . . .

WHAT... WHAT'S HAPPENIN
STEVE TREVOR NEVER
LIKE THAT! I MUSTN'T
HAPPEN... THIS WONDER
DELICIOUS THING -- MU
FIGHT IT! I'M WONDE
WOMAN... WONDER..
.WOMAN...
WONDER...

YOU MIGHT END UP TALKING ABOUT WORK DAY **AND** NIGHT.

YOU COULD BECOME DISTRACTED BY YOUR RELATIONSHIP AND START FORGETTING ABOUT WORK.

CO-WORKER CODEPENDENCE QUIZ

Dating is already a hazardous activity, but when you're dating a co-worker, the potential for disaster moves up to DefCon 2. You're spending all your time together; it's easy to get completely wrapped up. If you're even a tiny bit codependent, office dating is not for you. Take this quiz to find out.

Most of my work day is spent:

1. answering phone calls.

2. preparing financial forecasts.

3. sending text messages to my boyfriend, such as "I love you *this much,* and don't you forget it. *Ever.*"

At lunch, I usually:

1. eat at my desk.

2. go to the gym.

3. collect DNA from my beloved's sandwich crust so I can clone a replacement if he ever leaves me.

An appropriate gesture of affection is:

1. a hug.

2. a handmade card.

3. the utter destruction of my loved one's enemies.

SCORE: ANY 3s? YOU MIGHT WANT TO THINK ABOUT STAYING SINGLE FOR A WHILE.

BUT THAT NIGHT DIANA IS WAKENED FROM A SOUND SLEEP BY THE BUZZING OF HER MENTAL RADIO.

BUZZZZ-ZZZZ-ZZZZ-

GODS OF OLYMPUS- I'LL BET STEVE'S IN TROUBLE! I KNEW THAT GIRL WOULD START SOMETHING-

WITH FRANTIC SPEED DIANA TRANSFORMS HERSELF INTO **WONDER WOMAN.**

OH NO- **NO!** STEVE **MUST** NOT DIE - APHRODITE HELP ME GET TO HIM IN TIME!

EVEN WONDER WOMAN HAS HER MOMENTS.

OFFICE ROMANCE ETIQUETTE

If the attraction proves too powerful and you two decide to go for it, make your lives easier by discussing how you'll handle the situation. Have clear guidelines about what's expected and what won't fly. And spare your office mates any gooey squirmfests: save the terms of endearment for off-work hours, and limit public displays of affection to winks. No one wants to see your merger.

"THE GODDESS DIANA, STROLLING ONE DAY IN THE FOREST, CAUGHT A MAN LOOKING AT HER."

LOOK, GODDESS! A MAN IS GAZING ON THY BEAUTY!

HE MUST BE PUNISHED!

OFFICE SIDEKICKS

Instead of an office crush, why not recruit an office sidekick? You'll always have a companion for work functions and you won't have to buy her a present on Valentine's Day. Pick the co-worker you get along with best, and outfit her with a uniform. Anything will do, as long as her cape is shorter and her heels are lower (no upstaging). Then give your new sidekick a name, and you're an official awesome twosome.

GOOD OFFICE SIDEKICK NAMES:

COPY CAT

MISS FAX-IT

PENCIL NECK

THE TONER

WONDER WOMAN MAY WORK FOR THE SATISFACTION OF SAVING humankind, but most of us are in it for the perks and the paid time off. How often has the daily grind sapped your strength, depleted your mythical and gods-given energies, and made you feel not just mortal but subhuman? It's essential to recharge your batteries and get some rest and relaxation by taking a vacation or enjoying the occasional fringe benefit. Every working Wonder Woman needs a little retreat to Paradise Island from time to time (and remember, with most companies, the vacation policy is "use it or lose it"!).

HIDDEN BY A SHROUD OF MIST AND COMPLETELY UNCHARTED ON ANY MAP, PARADISE ISLAND IS AN UNSPOILED, NEARLY MYTHICAL UTOPIA WHERE YOU'LL FIND DELIGHTFUL AMENITIES:

PRISTINE BEACHES

ANCIENT TEMPLES

GREAT GREEK FOOD

SPA TREATMENTS (MASSAGE, MANI/PEDI, STRENGTH TRAINING)

AERIAL TOURS OF THE ISLAND BY INVISIBLE PLANE

AND MUCH, MUCH MORE!

PAID ADVERTISEMENT

TRY OUT THE UNIQUE LOCAL SPORTING EVENTS.

VISIT THE LOCAL ARTISANS FOR THAT SUPER SOUVENIR.

PARADISE ISLAND IS THE PERFECT PLACE
TO RELAX, REJUVENATE, AND LET YOUR HAIR
AND YOUR SUPERPOWERS DOWN. LEAVE
YOUR WORRIES AT HOME, AND ENJOY
YOUR VACATION WITH US!

THE AMAZONS ON PARADISE ISLAND
WELCOME YOU!

PAID ADVERTISEMENT

TREAT YOURSELF!

THE FIFTEEN-MINUTE VACATION

Can't get away? Treat yourself to one of these in-office mini-spa treatments.

Massage: Claim tendonitis, and the office ergonomist might give you a free shoulder rub.

Office Supply Facial: It's tempting to use rubber cement—it'll certainly tighten your skin, and goodness knows the fumes will relax you—but the potential for brain damage and clogged pores is just too high. Instead, using your jacket as a tent, steam your pores over a cup of hot herbal tea (not too hot—you don't want a steam burn) for a couple of minutes. Afterward, place the cool tea bags on your eyelids for five minutes to reduce puffiness.

Mani/Pedi: Give yourself a Wite-Out nail job.

R & R Down Under: And finally . . . there's always the under-desk mini nap.

BENEFITS

If you've played your cards right, you've scored full medical and dental coverage. This is actually two benefits in one, because not only are your office visits covered, but you get to miss work to go to them! So be sure to get regular checkups. A Wonder Woman knows maintenance is crucial to good health, good work—and good moods.

ONLY A FEW SHORT SECONDS DO THE *JUSTICE LEAGUE* MEMBERS LIE HELPLESS AND BEATEN. THEN A CHANGE COMES OVER THEM...

THANK HERA! I CAN FEEL MY SUCCESS FACTOR FLOWING BACK INTO ME!

JUST AS A BATTERY CAN BE RE-CHARGED--SO OUR INNER SELVES ARE BEING RECHARGED WITH OUR LOST VICTORY FORCE!

Be sure to avail yourself of any other goodies your office might offer, like transit vouchers, a parking spot, free snacks, health club membership, time-and-a-half pay, and an army of minions.

OTHER PERKS

Even better, taking care of yourself ensures you'll live long enough to enjoy your other benefits, like your stock options and 401(k). These are truly the cherry on the cake of your career. And if you want to have your cake and eat it too, you need to stay on top of them. Know where your investment funds are and what they're doing. If words like "IRA" and "capital gains tax" make your jaw clench and your brain shut off, not to worry: it's just math. You're a Wonder Woman! You can *certainly* handle a few decimal places. So open all those little envelopes the investment company sends you, read the financial pages, and consider attending shareholder meetings. Stay informed and involved, because "early retirement" is the most beautiful pair of words in the English language. And if your company doesn't offer the good stuff, consider working for The Justice League—they have a *great* pension.

WHAT WOULD YOU CHOOSE?

You're wearing a lot of hats and one *fabulous* tiara—enjoying life, doing an amazing job, and saving the world (yes, *again*). But even though the fate of the world may hang in the balance, you can do it—after all, you're a Wonder Woman!!